To:

....

From:

....

CHRISTMAS
A Gift for Every Heart

CHARLES F. STANLEY

THOMAS NELSON
Since 1798

Contents

1

When the Time Comes

God with You, Wherever You Are

What does Christmas mean to you? What memories come flooding back as you encounter the sights, sounds, and smells of the season? Who is it that you think about or wish to be close to as this time of remembrance commences?

It is different for each person, of course. The very first Christmas I can remember was when I was three. My father had passed away when I was nine months old, so my granddad, uncles, and aunts came to Danville, Virginia, during the holidays to see me and help my dear mother.

I recall it as if it were yesterday. They opened the trunk of their car, and it was filled with toys for me. I had never seen so many wonderful playthings. That was the most gifts I ever received for Christmas, and one thing was certain—I wanted to begin enjoying all of it as soon as possible!

My children, Andy and Becky, were the same way. They would spend the days leading up to Christmas examining their wrapped presents—reading the names on the tags, shaking the boxes, and trying to figure out what was in them. There was a thrill in their hearts that lit up their eyes. Then on Christmas morning, they wouldn't care about what we were going to have for breakfast or what was on television. They would wake up early and rush to the tree to find out what was inside those packages. They just couldn't wait to open everything and begin playing with all their new toys.

This is probably true of most children. They see beautifully wrapped presents under the tree and cannot wait to see what's inside. What treasures do they hold? What joy is hidden under the colorful paper and bows? They wouldn't think of simply admiring the packages and leaving them unopened.

Unfortunately, that is exactly what many people do at Christmastime: they overlook the greatest Gift that has ever been given, dwelling on the wrappings of the season rather than the supernatural blessing that it represents. In fact, after a while Christmas becomes just like many of the other days we celebrate—such as Thanksgiving, Labor

People overlook the *greatest Gift* that has ever been given, dwelling on the wrappings of the season rather than the supernatural *blessing* that it represents.

Day, Independence Day—with lots of shopping, gathering, and eating, maybe opening some presents and practicing special traditions. Of course there's nothing wrong with those other holidays or the ways we observe them, but the point is that we lose sight of the fact that Christmas commemorates an event unlike any other—the birth of the Savior.

> Human eyes are able to *behold* the exalted, omnipotent, all-knowing *Lord* of all creation!

Think about it. Why did the prophets, the New Testament writers, and even Christ's enemies give so much attention to Jesus' birth? It's for a good reason, of course—an important one. Because when God does something so tremendous and impactful, it is worth noting.

You see, Jesus' story really begins far before His birth. The gospel of John tells us, "In the beginning was the Word, and the Word was with God, and the Word was God" (John 1:1). Jesus was not created as you and I were. He is uncreated—the eternal God—without beginning from everlasting past and without end in the infinite future.

And because of that exceptional, extraordinary, eternity-altering moment when "the Word became flesh, and dwelt among us, and we saw His glory" (John 1:14), human eyes are able to behold the exalted, omnipotent, all-knowing Lord of all creation!

"They shall call His name *Immanuel*," which translated means, "*God* with us."

—MATTHEW 1:23

Thousands of years of fervent, desperate prayers to God and pleas for deliverance were answered the day Christ was born. It was not just the mere birth of a baby. It was not just a day that a great man appeared on the scene or that a significant treaty was ratified. It was the absolute shaking of the spiritual and physical realms when God Himself was incarnated—becoming one of us in order to carry out all the promises He'd given through the ages.

> God Himself was *incarnated*—becoming *one of us* in order to carry out all the *promises* He'd given through the ages.

Matthew affirmed, "All this took place to fulfill what was spoken by the Lord through the prophet: 'BEHOLD, the virgin shall be with child and shall bear a SON, and they shall call His name IMMANUEL,' which translated means, 'GOD with us'" (Matthew 1:22–23). This is the foundation upon which every bit of our hope and joy rests. It is the truth that *God is with us.*

I am convinced that the reason some find Christmas to be a very difficult time of year is because they have lost sight of this truth in the midst of all the ornaments, trappings, and wrappings of the season. They have good

KEEP YOUR *eyes* ON THE ONE WHO HAS *given* YOU ALL *things*.

reason, of course. The absence of loved ones, loneliness, financial pressures, unaccomplished dreams, and unmet expectations understandably crush our spirits during a season when we should be rejoicing. But this happens when we focus on relationships, possessions, activities, and disappointments instead of keeping our eyes on the One who has given us all things. We look to what we don't have instead of what cannot be taken from us.

I experienced this at one particular point in my life when I felt totally alone. Heaviness gripped my heart in such a consuming manner that I confessed it to God—I told Him that I was overcome with loneliness. As I spent time with Him that day, I sensed Him saying, "I am with you. I haven't left you. I'm here, and I'm not going anywhere." That still, small voice deep within my spirit encouraged me deeply. I recall leaving my prayer room overflowing with a fresh sense of hope. My circumstances had not changed, but my focus had—and that made all the difference.

"I am with you. I haven't left you. I'm here, and I'm not going anywhere."

And what I want you to see is that God's words to me that day were the very essence and reality of Christmas: He is with you. He loves you. He listens to the cries of your heart. When you are hurting, He is near to you and cares for you. When you are powerless, He gives you strength. When you are in despair, He brings His promises to mind and reveals the blessings He has planned for you. And when you feel disrespected, worthless, or inadequate, He reminds you that you are His, that He died for you, that He adores you, that He is your adequacy, and that He will never let you go.

This is why I want to encourage you this Christmas to focus on the hope of every heart: Jesus, our Savior. Unwrap the gift that was first given so long ago on that extraordinary night in the town of Bethlehem. Don't be distracted by the presents, the food, the activity, or the trimmings. Just look to *Immanuel*, God with us. Focus on His presence no matter where you are.

Because if you do, you will not only rediscover the absolute wonder of Christmas. You will also see how Jesus meets your every need.

Promises *of* God's Presence

The LORD is the one who goes ahead of you; He will be with you.
He will not fail you or forsake you. Do not fear or be dismayed.

Deuteronomy 31:8

"My presence shall go with you, and I will give you rest."

Exodus 33:14

"Do not fear, for I am with you;
Do not anxiously look about you, for I am your God.
I will strengthen you, surely I will help you,
Surely I will uphold you with My righteous right hand."

Isaiah 41:10

"I will not leave you as orphans; I will come to you."

John 14:18

"I am with you always, even to the end of the age."

Matthew 28:20

Hark! The herald angels sing,
"Glory to the newborn King;
Peace on earth, and mercy mild,
God and sinners reconciled!"

Joyful, all ye nations rise,
Join the triumph of the skies;
With th'angelic host proclaim,
"Christ is born in Bethlehem!"
Hark! the herald angels sing,
"Glory to the newborn King!"
Christ, by highest Heav'n adored;
Christ the everlasting Lord;
Late in time, behold Him come,
Offspring of a virgin's womb.
Veiled in flesh the Godhead see;
Hail th'incarnate Deity,
Pleased with us in flesh to dwell,
Jesus our Emmanuel.

Charles Wesley

2

Because Perfect
Isn't Possible

God, Your Redeemer

At Christmastime, how often do you find yourself thinking, "I want everything to be perfect"? Perhaps there is an important meal you are making, a special gift you are choosing for a loved one, or some event that you hope will go flawlessly. You do all you can think of to make sure everything is just right—putting a lot of pressure on yourself in the process. But then something goes wrong, a key part of your strategy goes awry, or someone reacts in a way you hoped he or she wouldn't.

In one fell swoop it feels as if you've failed. Christmas has been ruined.

If your Christmas plans ever fall short of what you've envisioned, take heart. Even the setting of Jesus' birth was far from ideal.

The place Mary laid

Jesus was far from

what a new mother

would want for her

sweet firstborn *child:*

a feeding trough.

The timing of the trip—mandated by Rome—was less than perfect: Mary was nine months pregnant.

The transportation was nowhere near adequate for a four-day, approximately ninety-mile journey: a donkey.

Accommodations in Bethlehem were less than perfect: a cave being used as a stable and, now, a nursery.

The place Mary laid Jesus was far from what a new mother would want for her sweet firstborn child: a feeding trough.

Too often, we get caught in the trap of thinking every detail of Christmas must be just so. The activities, decorations, and presents often become an all-consuming pursuit. But if we're honest with ourselves, one of the reasons we cover ourselves up with busyness is because there are certain things about ourselves we don't want to face or let on to others. Somehow, amidst all the activities, we still feel unsettlingly empty and inadequate. And so we are more drawn to the distractions of the season because—whether we realize it or not—we are intimidated by the thought of being less than what God and others expect us to be.

Thankfully, Jesus didn't come in such a profound way to walk among us because we had it all together. In fact, it was the moment that everything stopped being perfect—when our relationship with the Father was broken in the garden of Eden—that made it necessary for our Savior to come.

Maybe it surprises you that Adam and Eve play a role in the Christmas story. Well, it was in the garden of Eden that we first saw our need for a Redeemer.

You most likely know Adam and Eve's story from the book of Genesis. God created the first man and woman in His image and charged them to care for the world He had newly formed. Innocent of evil and free of sin, they had the privilege of walking with the Father daily in unhindered love and fellowship. And there was only one thing they were required to avoid: the Tree of Knowledge of Good and Evil.

God said, "From any tree of the garden you may eat freely; but from the tree of the knowledge of good and evil you shall not eat, for in the day that you eat from it you will surely die" (Genesis 2:16–17).

Sadly, the two disobeyed. They ate the fruit of the forbidden tree, and all of humanity has been affected ever since. Romans 5:12 explains, "Through one man sin entered into the world, and death through sin, and so death spread to all men, because all sinned." In other words, we all feel this alienation from God because we all bear the sin nature that began with Adam and Eve.

Immediately the couple knew they had done wrong, so they hid themselves from the One who loved them most. The Father had formed Adam and Eve for one purpose—and it's the same reason He so lovingly made you and me: He wants us to experience a deep, fulfilling relationship with Him. But Adam and Eve's fall ruined that possibility for all of us and set us on the path of separation from God and eternal death.

God wants us to *experience* a deep, fulfilling *relationship* with Him.

Imagine the terrible shame, regret, and hopelessness Adam and Eve must have felt being sent out of the garden and away from fellowship with God. I don't know how a soul bears that kind of guilt. No wonder they wanted to disappear—to hide from their mistakes and embarrassment. In some ways, we can all identify with Adam and Eve. We all disobey the Father, sin, and hurt others. Our actions damage relationships and keep us from the profound intimacy with God that we were created to enjoy. So we try to conceal both who we really are and the issues that weigh on our hearts.

But that is exactly the reason Jesus was born. God saw our condition and knew we wouldn't be able to handle it on our own.

You see, Christmas didn't happen *despite* Adam and Eve's fall; rather, Christmas occurred *because of* their terrible decision to do what they thought best instead of what God had commanded.

From the very beginning, Jesus has been the answer to humanity's worst mistake ever—because every other sin, bad decision, tragedy, atrocity, and heartbreak have flowed from the consequences of that one act of disobedience in the garden of Eden. Adam's sin broke our relationship with God; Jesus' sacrifice redeemed it.

From the very beginning,
Jesus has been
the answer.

The word *redemption* means "to purchase or buy back." In the world of commerce, the original owner could redeem—or rescue—something or someone he had lost by paying a certain sum for that item. And what did our redemption cost the Savior? We know from Hebrews 9:22 that "all things are cleansed with blood, and without shedding of blood there is no forgiveness." That's why the price for buying us back from the penalty of sin was the blood of a perfect sacrifice—the kind of offering only Jesus could make.

You certainly don't have to be *perfect* for *God* to love you.

Friend, do you see what all this means? Jesus paid the price for your sin. You don't have to hide, and you certainly don't have to be perfect for God to love you. It is Jesus who makes you holy and acceptable.

Now, if you don't know Jesus as your Savior—as the One who forgives your sins and loves you unconditionally—I trust you will accept Him now. You can tell Him in your own words or use this simple prayer:

Lord Jesus, thank You for choosing to leave heaven, to be born into this world, and ultimately to die on the cross in order to redeem me from my sins. Jesus, I am so grateful that You've taken that burden from me through Your perfect, sinless life. I accept You as my Savior and Lord. Thank You for forgiving me of all my sins and enabling me to be in relationship with You—something I could not do on my own. Help me to live in a way that pleases and honors You, my Redeemer and King. Amen.

If you've just received Jesus as your Lord and Savior, you've just made the very best decision you will ever make. There is absolutely nothing more important in this life and for eternity than having a personal relationship with God and understanding that Jesus is the One who makes you completely acceptable, perfectly holy, and totally worthy.

As I said before, the first Christmas was far from perfect for anyone—except God. He saw through the difficulties to the heart of Christmas—to the eternal purpose of redeeming us through the birth, life, and sacrifice of Christ. He does the same with you: He looks past all the imperfections to your heart of faith in His Son.

So whether this is your first or ninety-first Christmas with Jesus, resist the temptation to hide from Him through activities and other holiday-inspired distractions. If feelings of insecurity, insignificance, and inadequacy creep in, remember what He came to do. Embrace and celebrate the birth of Christ, your Redeemer. Don't torment yourself with expectations that everything must go flawlessly and stop trying to make every detail perfect. Instead, spend time with Jesus and invite His great love to transform your life. Rejoice that Jesus has taken away the burden to be perfect. And thank Him that His wonderful hope can be birthed in every situation and circumstance you face.

Christ's *wonderful* hope can be birthed in every situation and circumstance you face.

Promises *of* God's Redemption

You shall call His name Jesus, for He will
save His people from their sins.

Matthew 1:21

Jesus Christ the Nazarene, whom you crucified, whom
God raised from the dead . . . There is salvation in no one
else; for there is no other name under heaven that has
been given among men by which we must be saved.

Acts 4:10, 12

"Do not fear, for I have redeemed you;
I have called you by name; you are Mine!
When you pass through the waters, I will be with you;
And through the rivers, they will not overflow you."

Isaiah 43:1-2

As far as the east is from the west,
So far has He removed our transgressions from us.

Psalm 103:12

Oh, what joy for those
whose disobedience is forgiven,
whose sin is put out of sight!
Yes, what joy for those
whose record the LORD has cleared of guilt.

Psalm 32:1-2 NLT

O holy night, the stars are brightly shining;
It is the night of the dear Savior's birth!
Long lay the world in sin and error pining,
Till He appeared and the soul felt its worth.

A thrill of hope, the weary soul rejoices,
For yonder breaks a new and glorious morn.
Fall on your knees, O hear the angel voices!
O night divine, O night when Christ was born!
O night, O holy night, O night divine!

John S. Dwight

3

When Everything
Is Chaotic

God, Your Prince of Peace

*I*t is wonderful to know that we don't have to be perfect before God. But Christmas brings with it hectic schedules, tired loved ones, crowded malls, harried shoppers, and seasonal tasks that have absolutely nothing to do with Jesus' birth. A million details, people, events, and even crises pull us in as many different directions.

In all the hustle and bustle, where do you find silence and stillness? Where is your place of rest and tranquility in the midst of all the commotion?

Thankfully, the promise of a much-needed blessing appears throughout the Christmas story. Used more than four hundred times in Scripture, it is a word woven throughout the prophecies of Jesus' coming as a special gift to us from God.

That wonderful word is *peace.*

In speaking about the Savior, the prophet Isaiah reported, "A child will be born to us, a son will be given to us; and the government will rest on His shoulders; and His name will be called . . . Prince of *Peace*" (Isaiah 9:6).

Likewise, we read that, on the night Jesus was born, "there appeared . . . a multitude of the heavenly host praising God and saying, 'Glory to God in the highest, and on earth *peace* among men with whom He is pleased'" (Luke 2:13–14).

Surely this promise of peace is a welcome one—especially at Christmas when there is so much that can steal our inner tranquility. As soon as we are able to settle down, get some rest, and quiet our spirit, it seems as if some other request, demand, burden, or emergency rushes in. As quick as lightning, we lose the calm we worked so hard to find.

If you find Christmas a time of agitation and anxiety, you are certainly not alone. We tend to think that if we had enough money or the right connections, the holidays—all of life, in fact—would be much easier. Especially during the Christmas season, though, many look to wealth, and

His name will
be called . . .
Prince of Peace.

—*Isaiah 9:6*

possessions as the pathway to inner peace. They think that if they could just have that latest gadget, they would be happy. If they could only buy their loved ones those special gifts, they could maintain harmony in their household. Sadly, plans like these never work. Worldly goods can never fill our emptiness, give us worth, or restore broken relationships.

This is the inherent problem with the world's definition of peace: it is based on our limited human resources and therefore offers only temporary results. A momentary solution cannot reach down to the root of the issues causing our stress and anxiety, much less provide lasting relief.

My son, Andy, understood this principle from an early age. One evening while he was still in high school, he said, "Dad, thank you for not giving me everything I ever wanted." Of course this had me intrigued. I asked him why he felt this way. I will never forget his explanation.

Worldly goods can never fill our *emptiness*.

Andy replied, "Because many of my friends—well, their parents give them everything they want, and it has really messed them up. They think that's all there is to life. Thanks for teaching me what is truly important."

I was so grateful my son had learned the vital principle that peace, joy, and fulfillment come through Christ, not from anything this world offers.

So, as Christmas approaches, what can you do to maintain genuine tranquility despite the season's activities and pressures? What can you do to preserve harmony within yourself, with others, and, most importantly, with your heavenly Father?

Jesus shows us the way. He taught that we could have His profound inner peace in even the most chaotic situations. He told the disciples, "Peace I leave with you; My peace I give to you; not as the world gives do I give to you. Do not let your heart be troubled, nor let it be fearful" (John 14:27). Christ's tranquility is not based on circumstances; rather, it is a supernatural gift that we are blessed with when we walk with Jesus as our Lord and Savior.

Peace, *joy*, and fulfillment come through *Christ*, not from anything this world offers.

"Peace I leave with you;
My *peace* I give to you;
not as the world gives do I give to you.
Do not let your heart be *troubled*,
nor let it be *fearful* ."

—JOHN 14:27

I saw this kind of peace in a woman at church. Her son had been in a terrible accident, and he was not likely to live. When I spoke to her, I was struck by the calm, quiet assurance in her face and manner. She explained, "The peace of God has surrounded us like a holy cloud. He has given us this amazing peace that passes all our understanding."

Although she was experiencing a heartbreaking situation, it was obvious that the Father had enveloped her with His strength and assurance.

The good news is that Christ has made this kind of profound, abiding tranquility available to all of us who believe in Him. So how can you take hold of all He offers? How can you receive the "peace of God, which surpasses all comprehension" (Philippians 4:7)?

First, understand that the peace *of* God originates in our reconciliation *with* Him. Our entering into a relationship with Him marks the beginning of our ability to experience His true, heart-changing, supernatural tranquility.

The Greek word for *peace* is *eirene*, and it means "to bind together." When you trust Jesus as your Savior, He binds you to Himself for all eternity. You never need to worry about losing your salvation because Jesus made you right with the Father through His death on the cross—and no one can ever take that away from you. No matter what occurs here on earth, you can be absolutely confident of your right relationship with God and assured that you have a home in heaven.

But, second, we must also realize that harmony *with* the Father leads to the calmness of soul that can only come *from* Him. In other words, our choice to obey God enables us to experience the supernatural peace that He gives.

The peace of God, which surpasses all comprehension, will guard your hearts and your minds in Christ Jesus.

—Philippians 4:7

Of course, you may be wondering why you must submit to the Lord's plans in order to experience tranquility. You may feel you know what is best for your own life, so why listen to Him?

Remember, God understands you better than you comprehend yourself. He sees your potential and all that is possible through you. So when you head in a direction that is contrary to what you were created for or that could conceivably hurt you, His Holy Spirit will always prod you to return to His path because He only wants the very best for you.

But when you obediently walk in God's will, His wisdom, power, and love protect you and preserve your peace. What happens to you is like what happens during a raging ocean storm. The driving winds and rain may stir up tumultuous waves that no ship could survive. But if you descend beneath the surface several hundred feet, you find that the water is quiet, still, and calm. You wouldn't even know a tempest was thundering on the surface.

When people learn to walk in a strong relationship with Jesus, the storms that assail their lives don't upset the calm assurance within them. Deep within, they remain at peace, dwelling in the Almighty's holy presence,

Our *choice* to obey God
enables us to experience the
supernatural peace
that He gives.

Whatever your
circumstances . . .
God is always
completely able
and *willing*
to help you.

grateful for His protection, and trusting in His plan. Knowing that God is sovereign, they are at peace because they understand that nothing touches their lives outside of His authority, wisdom, and love.

Third, we must also embrace the fact that Christ takes full responsibility for our needs when we obey Him. Earthly peace is often based on worldly resources that can—and ultimately will— fail. So when we face situations beyond our abilities, talents, skills, and wealth, no wonder we feel overwhelmed, anxious, and discouraged.

God *understands* you better than you *comprehend* yourself.

But Jesus is called the *Prince of Peace* for an important reason. The Hebrew word for *prince* is *sar,* which means "commander, ruler, leader, or captain"—the one who overcomes all obstacles in order to accomplish his purpose. In other words, whatever your circumstances may be, God is always completely able and willing to help you. As a believer, you can calmly and joyfully trust Him, because you know that the One who is best able to give you victory in every situation will never leave you or forsake you.

Finally, understand that you will experience the Father's peace when you make your relationship with Him your top priority and nurture it every day. Only the Lord is able to calm your worries and drive out your fears. So whenever concerns creep up this Christmas, consider it Jesus' call to spend time with Him.

Why? Because when you spend time with the Lord, you realize that He's got everything under control and that He will work everything out for your good. And when you walk in the center of His will and learn to see your circumstances from His perspective, you can enjoy that deep, wonderful, supernatural tranquility that I just described.

In addition to experiencing the peace that comes only through the Father, you'll also be a calming presence to those around you. You'll be able to handle the conflicts that arise with greater grace, wisdom, and composure.

So this Christmas, instead of fretting about presents you must purchase, people you must please, and parties you must plan, think of the One you need most: focus on the Prince of Peace. In faith, surrender yourself to His loving care. Rest in His ability to help you. Let the peace of the Lord Jesus give you unshakable calm this Christmas season, and you will experience the rest, gladness, and hope He created you to enjoy.

The One who is best
able to give you *victory* in
every situation
will never leave
you or forsake you.

Promises *of* God's Peace

"These things I have spoken to you, so that in Me you
may have peace. In the world you have tribulation,
but take courage; I have overcome the world."

John 16:33

In peace I will both lie down and sleep,
For You alone, O LORD, make me to dwell in safety.

Psalm 4:8

The LORD will give strength to His people;
The LORD will bless His people with peace.

Psalm 29:11

You will keep him in perfect peace,
Whose mind *is* stayed on You,
Because he trusts in You.

Isaiah 26:3 NKJV

May the Lord of peace Himself continually grant you
peace in every circumstance. The Lord be with you all!

2 Thessalonians 3:16

It came upon the midnight clear,
That glorious song of old,
From angels bending near the earth,
To touch their harps of gold:
"Peace on the earth, goodwill to men
From heavens all gracious King!"
The world in solemn stillness lay
To hear the angels sing.

O ye beneath life's crushing load,
Whose forms are bending low,
Who toil along the climbing way
With painful steps and slow;
Look now, for glad and golden hours
Come swiftly on the wing;
Oh rest beside the weary road
And hear the angels sing.

For lo! the days are hastening on,
By prophets seen of old,
When with the ever-circling years
Shall come the time foretold,
When the new heaven and earth shall own
The Prince of Peace, their King,
And the whole world send back the song
Which now the angels sing.

Edmund H. Sears

4

When You Must Wait

God, Messiah in the Impossible

When you think about Christmases past, which has been the most memorable? Which meant the most to you? Which one has a special place in your heart?

Often, what makes an event or a gift at Christmas so unforgettable is how long you waited for it. Perhaps you were given a special present you had hoped for months to receive. Or it could be that you visited loved ones or a place you'd waited forever to see. Or maybe God simply answered a prayer that had been on your heart for as long as you can remember. Whatever it was, the anticipation of the much-awaited event made it even sweeter when it finally happened.

And perhaps you are waiting for something important today—requests you've presented to the Father this Christmas that require His loving

The *Lord* masterfully *orchestrates* history in order to *fulfill* His word to His people.

intervention. Whether you have been waiting days, weeks, months, or perhaps even years, the story of Christmas has something very special and important to teach you. And I trust that—regardless of how your situation may appear—this message will encourage you to wait with hope, anticipating your Father's wise and loving action on your behalf.

After all, Christmas is gloriously undeniable evidence that, no matter how long the delay, God *always* keeps His promises, sometimes in ways we could never have imagined. As we think about the birth of Christ, we can take courage in seeing how the Lord orchestrated history in order to fulfill His word to His people who, throughout the ages, had set their hope on Him.

Christmas is gloriously undeniable evidence that, no matter how long the delay, *God* always keeps His promises.

If you recall, the nation of Israel waited thousands of years for the birth of the *Messiah*, which means "Anointed One." In Jewish culture, priests and kings were anointed with oil to be sanctified for service. However, there would come One who was not anointed by men, but who was consecrated by God Himself to rule the kingdom in peace and justice and to deliver the people from all that oppressed them.

In order for the people of Israel to recognize the Messiah when He arrived, the Father provided hundreds of prophecies that distinctly, specifically, and perfectly pointed to Him. God did this so that when Jesus came to earth, people would have absolutely no doubt that He was the Anointed One they had been waiting for. As their Messiah, Jesus would release them from far greater oppression than any earthly empire could impose: He would deliver whosoever believed in Him from their eternal captivity to sin and death.

As we look back, the fulfilled promises of Christmas serve as an astounding testimony to God's sovereign control over all history and creation. But what we need to keep in mind is that the accomplishment of all these Old Testament prophecies happened according to God's timetable, not the timing anticipated by His people. In fact, the wait for the fulfillment of many of these promises must have seemed endless to those who eagerly watched for the Lord to act.

> The fulfilled promises of *Christmas* serve as an astounding testimony to God's *sovereign* control over all history and *creation.*

I think of Abraham and how the Lord said, "In your seed *all the nations of the earth shall be blessed*, because you have obeyed My voice" (Genesis 22:18). Abraham had to wait a very long time for his beloved first child, Isaac. In fact, Romans 4:19 tells us Abraham was "about a hundred years old" when Isaac was finally born. Think about that—a hundred years old and having his first child! Of course, God's promise that Abraham would be a blessing to all nations took even longer. Hundreds of years passed before it was uniquely fulfilled through his descendant Jesus, who blessed the whole world by providing all of us with salvation.

God's promise that Abraham
would be a blessing to all nations . . .
was uniquely fulfilled through
his descedant *Jesus.*

"The Lord God will give Him the *throne* of His father David . . . and His kingdom will have no end."

—*Luke 1:32-33*

In yet another promise, God said to David, "Your house and your kingdom shall endure before Me forever; your throne shall be established forever" (2 Samuel 7:16). Because David was faithful, not only would his family's rule last as long as the earth remained, but the Lord added a very special word: *forever*. God planned to achieve eternal goals through David's line. Once again, the Lord allowed centuries to pass, and the fulfillment of this prophecy seemed utterly impossible. Foreign conquerors came and went, and no king from David's line was on the throne.

But then came the astounding day when the angel Gabriel told Mary, "You will conceive in your womb and bear a son, and you shall name Him Jesus. He will be great and will be called the Son of the Most High; and *the Lord God will give Him the throne of His father David*; and He will reign over the house of Jacob forever, and His kingdom will have no end" (Luke 1:31–33). With the birth of Christ, God fulfilled His eternal promise to David.

Throughout the Old Testament, God revealed which family Jesus would belong to, how He would be born, where His birth would occur, and the manner in which He would die. The Lord even revealed through the prophet Daniel the time when the Messiah would arrive. Each prophecy of the Anointed One made His arrival more unique and specific, and every delay made it seem more improbable. How could any one man possibly meet all the details God had laid out? The birth of Jesus proves that the more impossible the situation, the more glory the Father receives when He brings it to pass perfectly.

The apostle Paul wrote, "When the fullness of the time came, God sent forth His Son" (Galatians 4:4). The sovereign Father carefully made all the necessary preparations and engineered countless details as He arranged for this holy night we call Christmas. And at the perfect time, God's providential hand brought about the extraordinary moment: Jesus' birth, which changed the course of human history and the eternal destiny of all of us who are believers.

I tell you this for a very important reason: Christmas is unmistakable evidence that you can take heart even in the most impossible situations and the most interminable delays, because God *always* fulfills His promises. It may appear from all outward circumstances that His plan for you has fallen apart or that there is no way for Him to bring about what He's pledged to provide for you. But the Lord delights in situations that look unworkable from a human standpoint because then, when He answers, you have no doubt whatsoever that it was God Himself who acted on your behalf.

CHRISTMAS IS
UNMISTAKABLE
EVIDENCE THAT
YOU CAN TAKE HEART
EVEN IN THE
MOST *impossible*
SITUATIONS . . .
BECAUSE GOD *ALWAYS*
FULFILLS HIS PROMISES.

So as you celebrate Jesus' birth, waiting for blessings that you long for, remember that throughout history *every single person* to whom the Lord made promises faced circumstances that seemed absolutely impossible to overcome and many prolonged delays. Furthermore, the prophecies the Lord made throughout the ages about the Anointed One seemed completely unattainable. But as our Messiah, Jesus perfectly fulfills every detail that God has spoken through His prophets over the centuries.

In other words, friend, the Lord has *never* failed any of those who trusted Him, and He will not let you down either. You can rest in the truth that God is faithful and able to accomplish all He has said He would do. Likewise, as your Messiah, Jesus has been specially anointed to help you, guide you, save you, and be with you in seasons of waiting.

So don't lose heart when you have to wait on God. Instead, remember the message of Christmas—and know for certain that the sovereign Lord of all creation, your heavenly Father, your Messiah and King, has heard your requests and will faithfully fulfill all of His promises to you in His perfect time.

Promises *of* God's Faithful Fulfillment

We have found the Messiah.

John 1:41

Not one word of all the good words which the LORD your God spoke
concerning you has failed; all have been fulfilled for you.

Joshua 23:14

I would have despaired unless I had believed that
I would see the goodness of the LORD
In the land of the living.
Wait for the LORD;
Be strong and let your heart take courage;
Yes, wait for the LORD.

Psalm 27:13-14

"So will My word be which goes forth from My mouth;
It will not return to Me empty,
Without accomplishing what I desire,
And without succeeding in the matter for which I sent it."

Isaiah 55:11

God has fulfilled this promise to our
children in that He raised up Jesus.

Acts 13:33

Come, Thou long expected Jesus
Born to set Thy people free;
From our fears and sins release us,
Let us find our rest in Thee.

Israel's Strength and Consolation,
Hope of all the earth Thou art;
Dear Desire of every nation,
Joy of every longing heart.
Born Thy people to deliver,
Born a child and yet a King,
Born to reign in us forever,
Now Thy gracious kingdom bring.

By Thine own eternal Spirit
Rule in all our hearts alone;
By Thine all sufficient merit,
Raise us to Thy glorious throne.

Charles Wesley

5

When You Feel Defeated

God, Sovereign over History

Romans 8:28 teaches, "We know that God causes all things to work together for good to those who love God, to those who are called according to His purpose." I trust you believe that truth today as you prepare to celebrate Christmas. No matter what is happening in your life—regardless of how challenging, overwhelming, or complicated it is—you can take courage because the sovereign God of all that exists is actively working for your benefit.

In fact, this is one of the beautiful lessons we can draw from Christmas: God often uses the very difficulties we experience in order to achieve His truly wonderful objectives. What appears to be a terrible defeat or setback is actually the Father carrying out His plans for us in a magnificent way.

So we can always have hope because the Lord rules supreme over the world, all people, all time, and every situation. And because He loves us, we know that if some adversity touches our lives, He has some good and eternal purpose in it.

We can see this beautifully illustrated as the Messiah's story unfolds throughout the tumultuous history of the nation of Israel.

This is one of the beautiful lessons we can draw from *Christmas*: *God* often uses the very difficulties we experience in order to achieve His truly *wonderful* objectives.

Although Israel had periods of obedience, prosperity, and peace, her past was marked with innumerable wars that were the direct result of the people's unfaithfulness to God. Eventually, because of the people's disobedience, the kingdom was divided: the ten northern tribes continued to bear the name *Israel*, and the two southern tribes were called *Judah*. The people then persisted in their idolatry until the Lord allowed the Assyrians to destroy the northern tribes, scattering the Israelites among the nations. Later, the Babylonians conquered the southern nation of Judah and deported her people as well.

Being so far from home, unable to understand the language and having to endure the pagan cultures of their captors, was both difficult and heartbreaking for God's people. But the Father did not abandon them— nor would He ever. Although from all outward evidence His great plans for the descendants of Abraham seemed to have completely fallen apart, in the unseen His powerful hand was working in a mighty way to bring about all He had promised them.

In fact, because of the adversity, many of the Jews in those foreign lands renewed their commitment to the Lord, strove to honor Him, taught their children to seek Him, and were cleansed of the idolatry that had plagued

The Father did not abandon them—nor would He ever.

them. And because they were so far from the holy temple, they established centers known as *synagogues,* where they could assemble for prayer and the study of Scripture—a development that would later become vitally important to the first Christians.

The people of Judah endured captivity for seventy years, which was a long time. But just as God had foretold through His prophets, He miraculously took them back to the promised land and enabled them to return to Jerusalem and rebuild the temple. The Lord's deliverance and the privilege of returning to their homeland made honoring God and preserving His Word even more important to His people.

Finally, the Father made the awesome proclamation that the Jews had waited so long to hear: "Behold, I am going to send My messenger, and he will clear the way before Me. And the Lord, whom you seek, will suddenly come to His temple" (Malachi 3:1).

In other words, their promised Messiah was coming! You can imagine the joy that filled their hearts.

But then God did something they never expected.

Just because the *Father* appears to be *silent* doesn't mean He has *forsaken* you—and He certainly isn't sitting still, doing nothing.

The Almighty was
preparing for the birth
of the *Savior.*

He grew quiet.

For four hundred years.

What happened? Had God forgotten them? Had the people finally made Him so angry that He had given up on them? Had He forgotten His promises about the Messiah?

It may have felt that way to them. They couldn't explain the Lord's silence or the troubles that continued to plague them.

Maybe you feel the same way in your situation today.

But always remember, just because the Father appears to be silent doesn't mean He has forsaken you—and He certainly isn't sitting still, doing nothing.

During those four centuries, the Almighty was preparing for the birth of the Savior. God was actively setting the stage for the good news of salvation to spread worldwide. And He was working through the very civilizations that oppressed the people of Israel.

For example, the Lord worked through the reign of conqueror Alexander the Great to make Greek the universal language of art, commerce, medicine, philosophy, and—eventually—the gospel. Scholars translated the Hebrew Old Testament into the *koine* or *common* Greek—a work known as the *Septuagint*. This made Scripture much more accessible, which was very beneficial in spreading the good news of salvation.

After the Greeks, the powerful Roman Empire conquered and ruled. The Romans laced their territories together with paved roads and strategically positioned legions throughout the realm to provide security so citizens could travel safely. Both the Roman roads and the relative peace (known as *Pax Romana*) ultimately enabled missionaries to go everywhere—preaching, teaching, and proclaiming that the Savior had come.

God was *actively* setting the stage for the *good news* of *salvation* to spread worldwide.

In other words, the empires that conquered God's people were not a mistake. Each one played a part in the Lord's perfect plan. Through them, believers came to have a common language, safe roads, and even synagogues through which they could more easily exchange information with Jewish communities throughout the Roman Empire.

So by the time Jesus rose from the dead, the known world had been prepared with important communication innovations that would become imperative for spreading the gospel.

It is truly inspiring when you consider everything God did to ready the world for Christ's birth—and the Lord achieved it all through the adverse circumstances the people of Israel faced.

In many ways, we can see this same principle illustrated in Joseph and Mary's lives. Wanting to tax the citizens, Caesar Augustus commanded that everyone in the inhabited earth return to his city of origin to register for a census. For Joseph and Mary, that meant a very wearying and uncomfortable ninety-mile journey from Nazareth to the city of Joseph's forefathers—Bethlehem—at the time when Mary was nine months pregnant.

By the time *Jesus* rose from the dead, the known world had been prepared with important communication innovations that would become imperative for spreading the *gospel*.

One might wish to fault Caesar Augustus or the Roman Empire for the problematic command. But from eternity past, the Lord had planned for the Roman emperor to issue the historic decree that would mean the fulfillment of the prophecy in Micah 5:2—that the Savior would be born in Bethlehem.

> God Almighty moved men, nations, and even the heavens . . . to make sure the *gospel* could be preached throughout the *world* once Jesus provided for our *salvation.*

God Almighty moved men, nations, and even the heavens to set the stage for the birth of His only begotten Son and to make sure the gospel could be preached throughout the world once Jesus provided for our salvation on the cross. The Lord did not miss one detail in His perfect plan.

The same God who choreographed all of these amazing circumstances to provide for your salvation is with you today. He works with unimaginably great power, wisdom, and love in every situation that affects your life. And He has a marvelous plan for you.

Friend, if the Father has allowed some adversity to reach you, you can be absolutely certain of one thing: He intends to use it in a manner that will

God is on His throne and *intimately* involved in the circumstances of your life.

benefit you. The Sovereign Lord of all history—who directs kings, removes nations, raises up empires, and even stops the sun in the sky—helps you today. God is on His throne and intimately involved in the circumstances of your life.

So don't despise the troubles you face or give in to discouragement. Rather, submit to God's will, trust in His promises, and look for His perfect provision. Allow this adversity to draw you into a deeper relationship with your heavenly Father and watch Him work out all the details for your good and His glory. I have no doubt you will be absolutely amazed at all He will do.

"You will be absolutely *amazed* at all God will do."

Promises *of* God's Sovereign Provision

"I know the plans that I have for you," declares the LORD,
"plans for welfare and not for calamity to give you a future
and a hope. Then you will call upon Me and come and
pray to Me, and I will listen to you. You will seek Me and
find Me when you search for Me with all your heart."

Jeremiah 29:11-13

The LORD will accomplish what concerns me;
Your lovingkindness, O LORD, is everlasting.

Psalm 138:8

He who did not spare His own Son, but delivered Him over for us
all, how will He not also with Him freely give us all things?

Romans 8:32

To Him who is able to do far more abundantly beyond all
that we ask or think, according to the power that works
within us, to Him be the glory in the church and in Christ
Jesus to all generations forever and ever. Amen.

Ephesians 3:20-21

O come, O come, Emmanuel,
And ransom captive Israel,
That mourns in lonely exile here
Until the Son of God appear.
O come, Thou Root of Jesse's tree,
An ensign of Thy people be;
Before Thee rulers silent fall;
All peoples on Thy mercy call.
Rejoice! Rejoice!
Emmanuel shall come to thee, O Israel.

John M. Neale

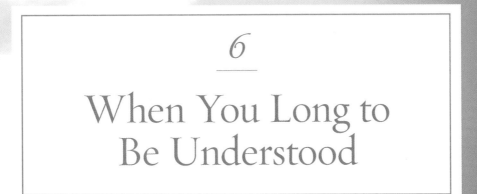

6

When You Long to
Be Understood

God as Man—A Sacrifice of Love

The gifts people give us can intentionally and unintentionally communicate a great deal about what they think of us. Some presents are very thoughtful, and they move us to the core of our being because of their kindheartedness and generosity. Other gifts may reflect love, but also reveal that the giver doesn't really know us. One Christmas my girlfriend gave me a sweater. It was very nice, and I knew she cared about me deeply. But that sweater just wasn't me. It wasn't what I liked or wanted—not by a long shot!

At times, we may wonder the same thing about the gifts and the plans the Father has for us. It is wonderful to know that our incomparable God—who is powerful, majestic, and wise, and whose hand guides all of creation—longs to help us, lead us, and love us. But we may question whether He understands the challenges we face every day and if He cares about the desires of our hearts. Does He truly know us?

God—THE *sovereign* LORD OF ALL THAT EXISTS—IS ACTUALLY *concerned* ABOUT THE ISSUES THAT *burden* US.

Perhaps we doubt that, in the grand scheme of things, God—the sovereign Lord of all that exists—is actually concerned about the issues that burden us. Does the Father genuinely comprehend what it's like to be us, to struggle as we do with our responsibilities and limitations? Does God realize the burdens we bear, the pain we suffer, or the rejection that haunts us?

I imagine that is what Mary wondered as well. A humble servant of the Lord, Mary was the woman specially chosen by God to give birth to the Savior of the world, and with great faith she submitted to God's plan for her life. But it was a privilege that would ultimately mean great sorrow. First, being *with* child and *without* a husband in ancient Israel most likely exposed Mary to terrible ridicule from those who didn't believe that her pregnancy was a God-appointed assignment. Jewish society scorned and condemned unmarried pregnant women, often stoning them to death.

At first, even Joseph, Mary's husband-to-be, didn't believe her story. Thankfully, he responded honorably: rather than subjecting Mary to public humiliation, he made immediate plans to divorce her quietly and send her away. But then an angel visited Joseph and confirmed that Mary's pregnancy was indeed the work of Almighty God. Believing the angel, Joseph took Mary to be his bride.

We can only imagine how lonely and rejected Mary must have felt through it all. In fact, we may wonder if it was really necessary for Mary, such a submissive servant of God, to face so much persecution when she was simply being obedient. No one in history has been or will ever be so highly favored as to carry the Savior—the Son of God—in her womb. And Mary loved the Lord, worshipped Him with all her heart, and trusted Him deeply. So why did she have to experience so much adversity? Why did such a godly young woman have to bear the burden of an unwed pregnancy?

No one in *history* has been or will ever be so highly favored as to carry the Savior—the Son of God—in her womb. So why did Mary have to experience so much *adversity?*

First, we know that the virgin birth was necessary in order to fulfill the prophecy in Isaiah 7:14 and distinguish Jesus as the Messiah: "Behold, a virgin will be with child and bear a son, and she will call His name Immanuel." But the virgin birth is also central to our salvation. Sin entered the world through Adam and spread to all mankind through his seed (Romans 5:12). Ever since then, the seed of the sin nature comes through the father. Yet, as we know, Jesus was miraculously conceived by the Holy Spirit (Luke 1:30–35)—not by a human father—so He did not receive the sin nature. Consequently, He was able to live a completely sinless life, which made Him the perfect sacrifice for us—the only and all-sufficient payment for our transgressions. So, yes, the virgin birth was absolutely necessary for our salvation.

But there is a second reason that the Father allowed Mary to experience so much difficulty, and that is because it had a profound and redemptive purpose in her life. We often view adversity as negative or destructive. But the truth of the matter is that hardships can have a very positive influence on a person's life and draw him or her even closer to God. In fact, in Romans 5:3–5, the apostle Paul wrote, "We . . . *exult* in our tribulations, knowing that tribulation brings about *perseverance*; and perseverance, *proven character*; and proven character, *hope*; and hope does not disappoint, because

Hardships can have a very *positive* influence on a person's life and *draw* him or her even *closer* to *God*.

the love of God has been poured out within our hearts through the Holy Spirit who was given to us."

Mary had an astoundingly great privilege: she would give birth to the Son of God. Certainly, as she raised Jesus, she would need perseverance, character, and hope. Anyone else may have become proud, ambitious, and conceited. But we know that Mary was a godly, faithful, and compassionate example to Jesus, a person who demonstrated trust in God in every aspect of her life. In other words, all the distress Mary endured before and during Jesus' birth prepared her for the challenges she would face as His mother.

There is a third reason the circumstances surrounding Jesus' birth were so difficult: our Savior had to become the Son of man so He could faithfully *represent us to the Father.*

We have spoken about how Christ's birth was truly unique because Jesus is *fully God.* In other words, Jesus shares all of the magnificent, eternal attributes of the Godhead. But Hebrews 2:17 tells us, "It was necessary for him to be made in every respect like us, his brothers and sisters, so that he could be our merciful and faithful High Priest before God" (NLT). In other words, in order to become our Savior, Jesus had to know what it was like

Our Savior had to
become the Son of man
so He could *faithfully*
represent us to the Father.

There, in the darkness
of a damp and dirty stable—
surrounded by the smells
and sounds of
animals—our *Savior*
entered the *world*.

to walk in our shoes. And in order to do so, He had to experience all the burdens and sorrows we carry.

I'm certain it was very distressing for Mary to leave her home and ride on a donkey right at the most uncomfortable time of her pregnancy. Mary and Joseph would have traveled nearly ninety miles to Bethlehem, most likely following the rough eastern bank of the Jordan River during a time of year that was frequently characterized by rainfall.

As the story goes, the young couple could find no place to stay when they arrived in Bethlehem. Joseph and Mary accepted the only shelter available: a stable that would have been a cave like those that still dot the hills around Bethlehem to this day.

There, in the darkness of a damp and dirty stable—surrounded by the smells and sounds of animals—our Savior entered the world. Rather than being clothed with fine and costly garments from the day of His birth, our beloved King was wrapped in strips of cloth and laid in a cattle feeder. Nothing about the setting suggested the true significance of the One who had been born.

We might wonder why God didn't provide Mary with a more dignified location to give birth. Why not give the Messiah a more comfortable place to rest His tiny newborn head?

As in everything else the Lord had planned, this unlikely setting was full of meaningful truths about the Savior.

Jesus' humble birth foreshadowed that He would suffer as we do—experiencing challenges and difficulties like those we face. Jesus was not rich, handsome, or especially appealing in any way. He knew the agony of being betrayed, insulted, and rejected. He understood what it felt like to be hungry, exhausted, lonely, tempted, bombarded by other people's needs, judged unjustly, and persecuted to the point of death.

And Jesus experienced pain deeper and more excruciating than you or I could ever face because on the cross He bore the sin and shame of every person who ever lived and who will ever live. He endured hardships just as every human being does, so that He could justly and compassionately represent us before the Father and faithfully serve as our Savior.

Jesus endured hardships and pain just as every human being does, so that He could *justly* and *compassionately* represent us before the Father and *faithfully* serve as our Savior.

But there is another aspect of Christ's birth that has profound significance, and that is the fact that He was born among the animals and laid in a manger. This event foreshadowed Jesus' ultimate sacrifice on the cross. Throughout Israel's history, the people had slain lambs as payment for their sins. The sacrificial system demonstrated that forgiveness of sin requires blood to be shed: one life was given for another.

However, merely covering sin rather than removing it completely, these animal sacrifices were never sufficient. A better offering was needed if all of our iniquity were to be removed once and for all. So from the moment of His birth, Jesus showed that He was the ultimate sacrifice—that He was "the Lamb of God who takes away the sin of the world" (John 1:29).

Why would Jesus endure all this? Why was the forgiveness of our sin so important to Him? The answer is this: "When the fullness of the time came, God sent forth His Son . . . so that He might redeem those who were under the Law, that we might receive the adoption as sons" (Galatians 4:4–5). Jesus saved us in order to make us a permanent part of His family. That's how much He loves us. That is why Jesus died on the cross: He gave His very life to forgive our sin, make us His own, and share in all that afflicts us.

Jesus *saved* us in order to make us a permanent part of His *family*.

Friend, God is not cold, distant, or disconnected from you. Your loving heavenly Father knows everything there is to know about you and longs to engage with you in a deep, meaningful, and satisfying relationship.

So as you consider the Christmas story, take heart by considering God's amazing plan and purpose. Think about the profound love Jesus exhibited when He took on flesh to identify with the struggles you face. Christmas offers you decisive evidence that your Savior knows exactly what it is like to be you.

As the Son of Man, Jesus mercifully reaches into the deepest, darkest part of your poverty, helplessness, and hopelessness because He wants to heal you fully and relate to you intimately. Your Savior is not surprised or repulsed by your wounds, fears, or failings. On the contrary, He knows all about them, which is why He has given so much—His very life—for you. This is why Jesus can truly be the hope of your heart.

So when trials come and the challenges set before you seem too great or too difficult, remember that just as God had a profound, eternal reason for all He allowed Jesus to endure, He also has a purpose for allowing hardships in your life. You don't have to wonder if He cares about the desires of your heart or comprehends the burdens you bear. You can be absolutely assured He does.

The Father may not tell you why you face certain things, but He will always be with you. Furthermore, He is in sovereign control of all that concerns you. And you can be completely confident that He knows exactly how you feel, understands you perfectly, and is always providing the very best gifts for you no matter what.

Promises *of* God's Comfort

The Spirit of the LORD GOD is upon me,
Because the LORD has anointed me
To bring good news to the afflicted;
He has sent me to bind up the brokenhearted,
To proclaim liberty to captives
And freedom to prisoners.

Isaiah 61:1

The LORD's lovingkindnesses indeed never cease,
For His compassions never fail.
They are new every morning;
Great is Your faithfulness.

Lamentations 3:22-23

I am convinced that neither death, nor life, nor angels, nor principalities,
nor things present, nor things to come, nor powers, nor height,
nor depth, nor any other created thing, will be able to separate us
from the love of God, which is in Christ Jesus our Lord.

Romans 8:38-39

The Lord shows compassion because of the greatness of his unfailing love.
For he does not enjoy hurting people or causing them sorrow.

Lamentations 3:32-33 NLT

Who is He in yonder stall
At whose feet the shepherds fall?
Who is He in deep distress,
Fasting in the wilderness?
Who is He the people bless
For His words of gentleness?
Who is He to whom they bring
All the sick and sorrowing?
'Tis the Lord! O wondrous story!
'Tis the Lord! The King of glory!
At His feet we humbly fall,
Crown Him! Crown Him, Lord of all!

Benjamin R. Hanby

7

Living Out Your "Thank You"

God—Your King, Priest, and Savior

*P*erhaps after reading about all that Jesus has done for you, a longing has begun to stir in your heart. Maybe a yearning is growing within you, a desire to give something back to the wonderful Savior who has sacrificed so much to redeem you, to restore your relationship with the Father, and to adopt you into His family.

Have you ever wondered what Christmas gift you could give to Jesus? What can you do to show gratitude for all that He has done for you? What can you give that would bless Him?

If you have ever pondered what the One who owns all of creation desires from His children, look no further. The Christmas story answers this question. We can learn a great deal from the Magi who followed the star to visit the newborn King.

What can you do to

show *gratitude* for all

that Jesus has

done for you?

The Magi—or wise men—were elite advisors from the East, possibly from somewhere near the city of Babylon. They were most likely astronomers who noticed an unusual star that indicated the birth of the long-expected Jewish King. But how did these men from far-off pagan lands know about the Messiah? And why would they even care that He had been born?

History shows that these Magi were probably descendants of people who had learned about the God of Israel and the promised Messiah from the prophet Daniel and other Jews the Babylonians had taken captive centuries earlier. Generations after Daniel, when the sign of the Jewish King finally appeared in the sky, the Magi understood its significance and made the long journey to Israel.

When the sign of the Jewish *King* finally appeared in the sky, the Magi understood its *significance.*

Arriving at the house where Jesus was, these men fell to the ground in humble worship and presented Him with gifts of gold, frankincense, and myrrh. From our perspective, their offerings may seem unusual for a baby, but Jesus was no ordinary child. These gifts symbolized who Jesus was and what He had come to do.

First, *gold* may not seem like a fitting gift for a child born into the household of a lowly carpenter. But in the ancient world, gold was given to show honor and esteem. It was a gift befitting a monarch, and that's exactly what Jesus is—our faithful and all-powerful King.

In fact, when Pilate asked Him if He was the King of the Jews, Jesus told him, "You say correctly that I am a king. For this I have been born, and for this I have come into the world" (John 18:37). Jesus is the heir to King David, whose "kingdom will have no end" (Luke 1:33). Indeed, we know Jesus as the almighty King of kings and Lord of lords who will reign triumphantly in eternity (Revelation 19:16).

Gold was a *gift* befitting
a monarch,
and that's exactly what
Jesus is—our *faithful*
and *all-powerful* King.

Frankincense, the second gift, played an important role in Jewish temple worship. When the priests sprinkled it on the burning coals of the golden altar, the fragrant smoke rose upward, symbolizing the offering of their prayers to God. The frankincense, therefore, pointed prophetically to Jesus' role as our Great High Priest.

In Latin, the word for *priest* means "bridge builder," and that is exactly what Jesus did for us: with His death on the cross, He spanned the gap between holy God and sinful humanity. As our High Priest, Jesus not only reveals the Lord to us, but He also faithfully represents us to the Father and intercedes on our behalf (Hebrews 7:25). Because of Jesus, we can "draw near with confidence to the throne of grace, so that we may receive mercy and find grace to help in time of need" (Hebrews 4:16).

Frankincense . . . pointed prophetically to Jesus' role as our Great High Priest.

Perhaps the final gift—*myrrh*—says the most about what Jesus came to earth to do. Myrrh was a costly perfume used primarily in burials. In the ancient East, myrrh was sprinkled on linen burial cloths in order to mask the odor of decay.

This gift spoke prophetically of Jesus' death on the cross and His role as our Savior. He came to earth to give Himself as the perfect sacrifice for our sins, laying down His life so we would not be eternally separated from the Father.

This gift of myrrh spoke prophetically of Jesus'
death on the cross and His role as our Savior.

The Magi's gifts to Jesus—the King of kings, Great High Priest, and Savior—suggest what we can offer to Jesus. We can honor our Lord by giving Him a heart that:

· *Acknowledges Jesus as our King of kings,* the One who alone is worthy of our complete obedience, loyalty, and respect.

The *best* gift you can give to Jesus is a life devoted to Him.

· *Reveres Jesus as our Great High Priest* who faithfully reveals God to us and represents us before Him.
· *Trusts Jesus as our Savior* who made the ultimate sacrifice to save us and reconcile us to the Father.

In other words, the best gift you can give to Jesus is a life devoted to Him. Because He is your *sovereign King*, you do whatever He calls you to do, whether you understand the purpose of His instructions or not. Because Jesus is your *wise High Priest*, you have faith in Him to teach you the way you should go even when the path seems unclear. And because Jesus is your *merciful and loving Savior* who paid such a high price for you, you trust Him to lead you in the very best manner possible even when you must face adversity.

Now perhaps you are thinking, *Well, that's fine. But I'm no wise man, Magi, or leader. What can I possibly do to serve God?* Friend, you don't have to be any of those things for the Father to work through you in a mighty way.

Remember that the first people to hear and share the news that the Messiah had come weren't the rulers, the priests, or the prophets. They were the shepherds. Luke 2:8–10 tells us this:

> There were some shepherds staying out in the fields and keeping watch over their flock by night. And an angel of the Lord suddenly stood before them, and the glory of the Lord shone around them; and they were terribly frightened. But the angel said to them, "Do not be afraid; for behold, I bring you good news of great joy which will be for all the people."

The shepherds were the first to hear that Jesus had been born. God sent the holiest of birth announcements to ordinary fellows—to men without wealth, power, or social standing. In fact, the Jews of the day considered shepherds to be outcasts because their work with the sheep made them ceremonially unclean. Those shepherds may have wondered if their lives counted for anything—and God's resounding answer to them was yes!

The Lord did not choose great orators, leaders, wise men, or officials to proclaim the good news of Jesus Christ that night. He chose the shepherds. Why? Because they were people just like you and me. And when they heard the joyful tidings, they didn't worry about what people would think of them or how the situation might look. The shepherds just knew that their news that the Messiah had finally arrived would give people hope. So wherever they went with their flocks, they announced that the Savior had been born in Bethlehem.

Don't miss the message here: it doesn't matter who we are. What God wants most from us is that we love Him, worship His holy name, and tell others about the wonderful salvation He has provided for us.

Those shepherds did not detract from the gospel because of their lowly estate; rather, they became *part of* the beautiful message that the Savior came to reach *all of us* no matter how humble or lowly we are in society's eyes. After all, God Himself is the One who gives us our hope, our identity, and our worth.

Christmas is a time of expressing love—God's love—to the people around you, and there is no better way to do so than to tell them about all Jesus did for them. So, to honor the Lord this Christmas and to live out your "thank You" to Him, proclaim the good news of salvation to the people you know. Honor Christ in your heart as your King, High Priest, and Savior. Share the hope He provides with everyone around you. Because, surely, Jesus is the best Gift that has ever been given.

WHAT GOD
WANTS MOST FROM
US IS THAT WE ... TELL
OTHERS ABOUT THE
WONDERFUL
salvation
HE HAS PROVIDED
FOR US.

Promises About Gifts *to* God

You do not desire a sacrifice, or I would offer one.
You do not want a burnt offering.
The sacrifice you desire is a broken spirit.
You will not reject a broken and repentant heart, O God.

Psalm 51:16-17 NLT

"He who offers a sacrifice of thanksgiving honors Me;
And to him who orders his way aright
I shall show the salvation of God."

Psalm 50:23

He has told you, O man, what is good;
And what does the LORD require of you
But to do justice, to love kindness,
And to walk humbly with your God?

Micah 6:8

"LOVE THE LORD YOUR GOD WITH ALL YOUR HEART, AND
WITH ALL YOUR SOUL, AND WITH ALL YOUR STRENGTH, AND
WITH ALL YOUR MIND; AND YOUR NEIGHBOR AS YOURSELF."

Luke 10:27

We three kings of Orient are;
Bearing gifts we traverse afar,
Field and fountain, moor and mountain,
Following yonder star.
O star of wonder, star of light,
Star with royal beauty bright,
Westward leading, still proceeding,
Guide us to thy perfect light.
Glorious now behold Him arise;
King and God and sacrifice;
Alleluia, Alleluia,
Sounds through the earth and skies.

John H. Hopkins

8

Unwrapping the Gift

God with Us as We Go

At the beginning of this book, I told you about a Christmas when I was three years old and my granddad, uncles, and aunts came to Danville, Virginia, and blessed me with many gifts. That was a wonderful time.

But after that very special Christmas, Mother and I had many lean years. We faced many disappointments and trials, and we often had very few presents to open at Christmas, if any at all. But one thing is certain: through both the lean times and plentiful seasons, God's gift of His Son has become more precious, real, and wonderful to me as time has gone by. The more I unwrap the reality of His awesome provision, the more joy and satisfaction I receive and the closer to Him I grow. My prayer is that you will discover the same to be true this holiday season and every day of your life.

Friend, obligations and tasks will always call for your attention and try to distract you from the true meaning of this blessed season. And whether you're overwhelmed by activities, challenges, or loneliness, if your eyes aren't fixed on Jesus, it's likely that you're feeling somewhat lost this Christmas. But the awesome gift of joy that God gives is that *He is with you*! And if you keep your attention on Him, He will guide you through every situation and circumstance you encounter.

One winter when I was in Colorado, I saw a perfect example of the importance of having the right focus. I recall driving down a snow-lined road on a beautiful sunny day, looking at the mountains that rose up around me.

God's gift of His Son has become more *precious*, real, and *wonderful* to me as time has gone by.

I thought, *This is a picture of the way life is.* There are always peaks we have to climb. Most of the time the path isn't as clear as we'd like it to be. We come to valleys, blind turns, and obstacles that obstruct our view of the road ahead. The only way we can avoid being lost is to focus on the mountain summit—and continue heading toward it.

Jesus wants to be that mountain summit for us. He wants us to keep our eyes focused on Him every day of our lives. As long as we do this, we will walk in His ways and avoid running astray. Like a compass, He is faithful to show us what our next step should be.

Jesus wants to be the mountain *summit* for us.

If you keep your attention on Jesus, He will *guide* you through every situation and circumstance you encounter.

But perhaps you're thinking, *Can I really trust Jesus to guide and direct me?* You absolutely can. Because whatever is ahead, He is everything you need.

Remember, Jesus is *Immanuel*: He is God with you. The indescribably awesome, infinite Lord of all that exists took on a form like ours and dwelt among us. Now, through His Holy Spirit, He is with you in every circumstance you will ever encounter. Therefore, you are never alone. Regardless of where you are or what you experience, you are assured of Jesus' wonderful, powerful, loving presence.

Whatever is ahead,
Jesus is *everything* you need.

Jesus is your *Redeemer* who has done for you what you could never do for yourself. He has reconciled you to the Father and has broken the hold sin and death had over you. Because Jesus has defeated these, your greatest foes, you can rest in His constant presence with you and trust in His perfect provision for you.

Jesus is your *Prince of Peace.* Even if your schedule becomes more hectic and responsibilities increase during this blessed season, you are assured tranquility in your relationship with Christ. He can speak solace and calm into your circumstances even when everything around you is in chaos.

Jesus is your *Messiah,* the One specifically anointed by the Father to lead you wisely and faithfully. He is the answer to every prophecy: "All of God's promises have been fulfilled in Christ with a resounding 'Yes!'" (2 Corinthians 1:20 NLT). And though He may delay, He assures you that certainly God "acts in behalf of the one who waits for Him" (Isaiah 64:4).

Jesus is the *King of kings and Lord of lords.* He is the sovereign Ruler over all that exists, over all history and creation. No problem or foe is too large or daunting for Him, and you can always trust that He will act in your best interest—with love, grace, and wisdom.

Jesus is the *Son of Man,* the perfect *Lamb of God,* and your *Great High Priest.* He is the sinless One who shares in your humanity yet bridges the gap between you and the Father. Jesus ushers you into a relationship with Him and teaches you His ways. He makes intercession for you, understands your weaknesses, and has the ability to meet every need you will ever have. Therefore, there is no one better to teach you how to live or to comfort you when you are hurting.

Jesus is your Savior. His is the only payment for the forgiveness of your sins that is absolutely acceptable to God, and His sacrificial offering is perfect, priceless, and everlasting. And this is the joy you can have before God: since the Father was willing to pay the high price of His only Son to purchase your redemption, you can be absolutely confident that He will always give you His very best. As Romans 8:32 testifies, "He who did not spare His own Son, but delivered Him over for us all, how will He not also with Him freely give us all things?"

So what is your focus this Christmas? What are you spending your time and energy trying to do? I trust that if your faith should waver and you begin to feel lonely, overwhelmed, lost, exhausted, or empty, you will realize that it's time to look to the hope of every heart, to the only One who can fulfill all your needs.

Jesus is worthy of your focus, worship, and praise at Christmas and always. He is your Prince of Peace, Messiah, Great High Priest, King, and Redeemer. He faithfully delivers you from all your bondage and burdens, and He is with you wherever you go and will sustain you no matter what you face.

Since God was willing
to pay the high price of His
only Son to purchase your
redemption, you can be *absolutely*
confident that He will
always give you His very *best*.

So I pray that during this Christmas season—and every one to follow—Jesus Christ will be foremost in your thoughts, your comfort in times of loneliness, your refuge in the storm, the focus of your life, and your delight always.

May Jesus bless you greatly as you seek His face. And may your heart overflow with His love, joy, and hope as you celebrate His glorious, incomparable, and wonderful birth this Christmas.

O come, all ye faithful, joyful and triumphant,
O come ye, O come ye, to Bethlehem.
Come and behold Him, born the King of angels;
Sing, choirs of angels, sing in exultation;
O sing, all ye citizens of heaven above!
Glory to God, all glory in the highest.
Yea, Lord, we greet Thee, born this happy morning;
Jesus, to Thee be glory given;
Word of the Father, now in flesh appearing.
O come, let us adore Him,
O come, let us adore Him,
O come, let us adore Him,
Christ the Lord.

John F. Wade

Jesus is *worthy* of your focus, worship, and praise at Christmas and *always*.

Promises About God's Guidance

Be strong and courageous! Do not tremble or be dismayed,
for the LORD your God is with you wherever you go.

Joshua 1:9

I will instruct you and teach you in the way which you should go;
I will counsel you with My eye upon you.

Psalm 32:8

Trust in the LORD with all your heart
And do not lean on your own understanding.
In all your ways acknowledge Him,
And He will make your paths straight.

Proverbs 3:5-6

It is God who is at work in you, both to will
and to work for His good pleasure.

Philippians 2:13

I can do all things through [Christ] who strengthens me.

Philippians 4:13

Joy to the world, the Lord is come!
Let earth receive her King;
Let every heart prepare Him room,
And heaven and nature sing,
And heaven and nature sing,
And heaven, and heaven, and nature sing.
Joy to the world, the Savior reigns!
Let men their songs employ;
While fields and floods, rocks, hills, and plains
Repeat the sounding joy,
Repeat the sounding joy,
Repeat, repeat, the sounding joy.

Isaac Watts